BURIAL PLACES

Discover Stone, Bronze and Iron Age Britain

Written by John Malam

WAYLAND

CONTENTS

STONE, BRONZE AND IRON

In 1816, a Danish man called Christian Thomsen was putting on a display in a Copenhagen museum. There were hundreds of prehistoric objects for the display and he wanted to put them in age order — but he didn't know how old each object was.

Thomsen decided to split the objects into three different groups depending on what material they were made from: stone, bronze and iron. Since stone is a natural material that is easy to work with, he thought stone objects would be the oldest. Bronze is softer than iron, so he placed bronze objects next and iron ones last.

This system became known as the Three Age System, and it's still used today.

The Three Age System in Britain

Flint cutting tool

Stone Age
(800,000 years ago to 2,300 BCE)
Tools, weapons and other objects were made from pieces of stone, especially flint.

Bronze Age
(2,300 BCE to 800 BCE)
Stone was replaced by metal. Copper was the first metal used. Then came a harder metal called bronze.

iron spear

Bronze dagger

Iron Age
(800 BCE to 43 CE)
Bronze gave way to iron, an even harder metal.
The Iron Age ended in 43 CE, when the Romans invaded Britain.

The Stone Age is divided into three periods:

1. Old Stone Age
or the Palaeolithic
800,000 to 10,000 years ago
The first people lived in Britain. Much of this period is called the Ice Age, because sheets of ice covered most of the land.

2. Middle Stone Age
or the Mesolithic
10,000 years ago to 4,000 BCE
The ice melted and groups of hunter-gatherer people moved across Britain.

3. New Stone Age
or the Neolithic
4,000 BCE to 2,300 BCE
The time of the first farmers and villages in Britain.

THE TIME BEFORE HISTORY

People first arrived in Britain about 800,000 years ago. The objects they left behind allow us to discover what their lives might have been like, and how they changed over time.

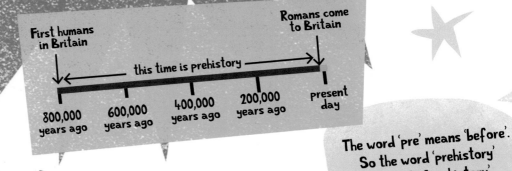

First humans in Britain

Romans come to Britain

this time is prehistory

800,000 years ago | 600,000 years ago | 400,000 years ago | 200,000 years ago | present day

The word 'pre' means 'before'. So the word 'prehistory' means 'before history'.

What is prehistory?

In 43 CE, a great army from the Roman Empire landed in Britain. They brought their lifestyle, traditions and knowledge with them. One of the things they brought was writing. They wrote down the events that happened, and from this point on recorded events are known as 'history'. Before the Romans arrived, there was no written language in Britain. This time is known as prehistory.

Reconstruction of an Iron Age roundhouse

Digging for clues

As there are no written accounts, the only way to find out about prehistory is by looking for prehistoric things, which are often buried underground. These might be objects such as stone beads or bone tools, forgotten or lost by people who lived thousands of years ago. People who study these objects are called archaeologists.

Neolithic flint arrowhead

PREHISTORIC TOMBS

There is evidence of prehistoric life all over Britain and Ireland. Wherever there were people, there are burial places — because people took great care of their dead. This map shows where some of the prehistoric tombs are to be found.

MAES HOWE

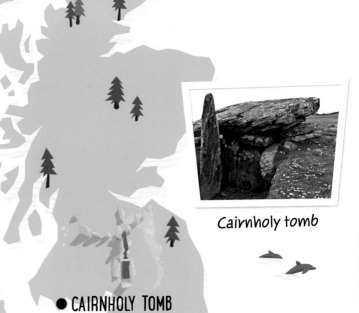

Cairnholy tomb

● CAIRNHOLY TOMB

● WETWANG SLACK

BROWNSHILL DOLMEN ●

PENTRE IFAN BURIAL CHAMBER ●

WEST KENNET ●

● SILBURY HILL

● LEXDEN TUMULUS

BUSH BARROW

LANYON QUOIT ●

Brownshill dolmen

TOMBS FOR THE DEAD

The remains of prehistoric people are buried inside tombs all across Britain. Archaeologists have explored these resting places of the dead and have discovered much about ancient burials.

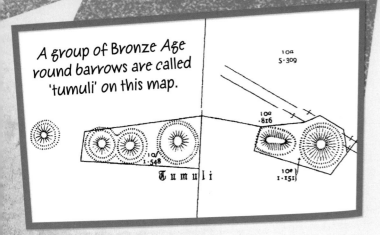

A group of Bronze Age round barrows are called 'tumuli' on this map.

A Bronze Age tomb on the Isles of Scilly, off the southwest coast of England.

Different names

Archaeologists call prehistoric tombs 'barrows'. It comes from an Old English word meaning 'hill'. The word 'tumulus' can also be used, or 'tumuli' if there's more than one mound. It comes from a word in Latin meaning 'mound' or 'hill'. Look out for it on maps!

Burying the dead

Archaeologists hardly ever find complete human skeletons inside Neolithic tombs. Instead, they find organised piles of bones belonging to many different people.

Archaeologists think that when somebody died, their body may have been left in the open air until it became a skeleton – and only some of its bones were then taken into the tomb. The most important bones, like skulls, may have been taken outside the tomb for ceremonies and then replaced.

Bronze Age people began to burn most dead bodies on very hot fires until only small pieces of bone remained, which were picked up and buried.

In the Iron Age, some dead bodies were buried inside barrows, some were cremated, and some might have been left in the open air to rot away before being buried in ditches.

Belas Knap Neolithic long barrow is in the Cotswold Hills, England.

Tomb types

Prehistoric people had different burial styles depending on where and when they lived. These are the main types of tombs they made:

Megalithic tombs
built in the Neolithic period

The word 'megalithic' means 'big stones'. These tombs were chambers covered by a mound or cairn of smaller stones.

Passage graves
built in the Neolithic period

These tombs have a passage leading to one or more chambers. They were covered with a cairn of stones.

Round barrows
built in the Bronze Age

These tombs look like small, round hills. They usually don't have passages or chambers inside them. Instead, they are often made from solid earth.

Long barrows
built in the Neolithic period

These are long mounds of earth. Some have passages and chambers or rooms inside them made of stone or timber.

THE FIRST BARROW BUILDERS

Even though they were built thousands of years ago, many prehistoric barrows are still remarkably intact. Today we can go inside some of these silent tombs, just as our prehistoric ancestors did.

Polished stone axe

A time of change

During the Neolithic, or New Stone Age, period, prehistoric people in Britain changed their way of life. They slowly stopped being hunter-gatherers, wandering across the land in search of food, and began to settle down and live in villages.

Neolithic people were the first to do several things in Britain. These included farming (of both crops and animals), living in villages, making pottery and building tombs.

Archaeologists think Neolithic people in southern Britain lived in houses like this.

Neolithic long barrows

The first prehistoric tombs in Britain were built in the Neolithic period. Some Neolithic tombs, called 'long barrows', are found mainly in the south of England. They look like long, low mounds. Most of the mounds are between 25 m and 60 m long, but they can be shorter or longer than this. A few are more than 100 m long!

Long barrows were made by digging two deep ditches opposite each other, a short distance apart. The soil that came out of them was piled up in the middle to make the mound. Some mounds were rectangles, but others were made with a tapering shape – they were wide at the front end and became narrower towards the far end.

Front entrance

Side entrance

The front 'entrance' of Belas Knap long barrow is false – the side entrances are the real way to get inside.

Stone passages and chambers inside a Neolithic long barrow.

Two types of long barrow

Some long barrows had passages and chambers made from stone. The builders piled earth on top to make the mound. These are called 'chambered long barrows' and you can still walk inside them today.

Other long barrows had chambers made from wood. Over the centuries the wood has rotted away and soil has filled the spaces. These long barrows are called 'earthen long barrows' because today they are just solid earth.

WEST KENNET

The West Kennet long barrow is a massive Neolithic tomb in Wiltshire, southwest England. Prehistoric people buried their dead inside it, and archaeologists have found some of their ancient bones. This great tomb has quite a story to tell.

Passage and side chamber inside the West Kennet long barrow.

Building the burial chambers

About 5,600 years ago, Neolithic people decided to build a big tomb. Heavy blocks of rough stone were dragged to the building site, some from about 32 km away.

Neolithic tomb builders moved the stones around until they had made a passage about 13 m long. It had five small chambers leading off it which were the burial chambers for the dead. Blocks of stone were placed on top to make a roof.

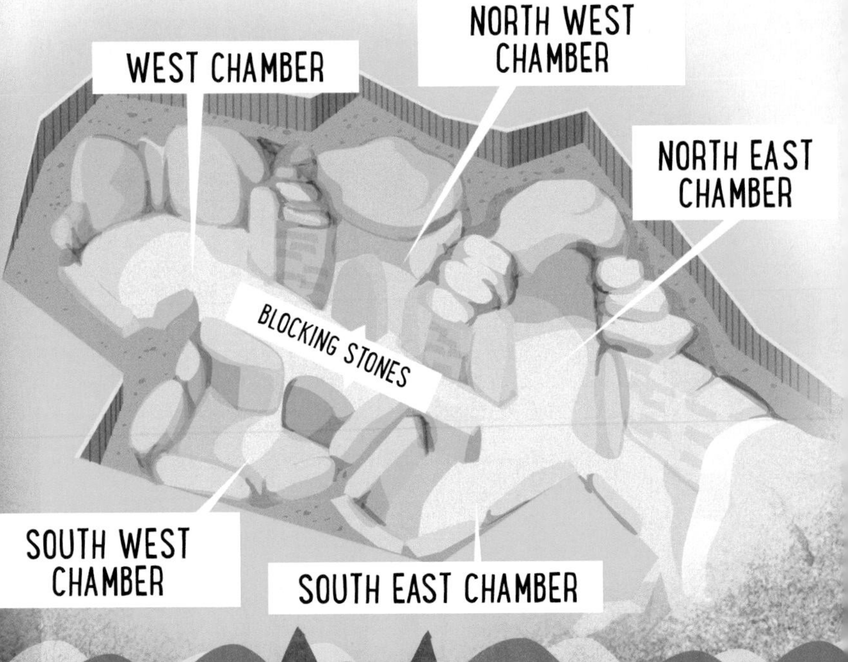

NORTH WEST CHAMBER

WEST CHAMBER

NORTH EAST CHAMBER

BLOCKING STONES

SOUTH WEST CHAMBER

SOUTH EAST CHAMBER

Making the mound

After the burial chambers were finished, the builders covered them over with a huge mound. To do this, they dug two ditches deep into the chalk bedrock, one on either side of the tomb. The chalk and earth from the ditches was used to make the mound – but it didn't just cover the burial chambers.

The builders carried on piling up the chalk and earth into a long, tapering mound. By the time they stopped, the mound was about 100 m long and 20 m wide, with ditches on either side almost 4 m deep!

Antler pick

To dig the ditches for the West Kennet long barrow, the builders used picks made from the antlers of red deer. Antler picks loosened up the hard chalk bedrock, and the rubble was then put into baskets which were emptied out to make the mound.

Bright white mound

The West Kennet long barrow must have been a dazzling sight. Because the mound was made from chalk rubble it would have appeared bright white, and could have been seen from far away. Today, the great mound is covered in grass.

The huge blocking stones that were put at the front of the West Kennet long barrow after it had gone out of use.

Out of use

After being used for about 1,000 years, the West Kennet long barrow went out of use and no more people were buried inside it. No one knows why this happened. The burial chambers were filled with chalk rubble and then blocked with stones. The passage was also filled with rubble, and huge stones were set up at the front to block the entrance.

HOW WERE LONG BARROWS USED?

When archaeologists look at tombs from other eras they usually find human bones laid out neatly, as if the body had been left untouched. But inside Neolithic long barrows, most of the time they find loose bones that are all mixed up rather than complete skeletons. Why?

Shared tombs

Tomb building involved heavy labour – it was hard work and took a long time. With so much to do, archaeologists think the building work must have been shared by several groups of people. Perhaps they were members of the same family, or belonged to the same clan or tribe. The finished tomb belonged to them all, and over the years it was used for the dead bodies of the local community.

Reconstruction of people gathering at the entrance to a Neolithic long barrow, where a body will be laid to rest.

Skulls, leg bones and arm bones piled up inside a Neolithic long barrow.

Moving the bones around

After death, prehistoric people visited the tombs and moved the bones of the dead around. We know this because archaeologists have found skulls, long bones and backbones gathered together into piles.

Sometimes bones are found that are still joined together, such as the bones of a hand or an arm. This shows the bones still had muscle and flesh holding them together when they were moved. It must have been a messy and smelly job!

Bones may have been moved when a new body was put inside the tomb, tidying away old bones to make room for it. Or perhaps the bones of the dead were brought out of the tombs into the 'land of the living', before being returned to the 'land of the dead' inside the tomb.

Flint arrowhead

One of the last people buried inside the West Kennet long barrow was an old man. For some reason his bones had not been moved around, and his skeleton was almost complete when found. His left arm had been broken, and amongst his throat bones archaeologists found a flint arrowhead. These two clues suggest the man had been killed.

Leaf-shaped flint arrowhead

MEGALITHIC TOMBS

In some places Neolithic people built megalithic tombs, which were chambers made from huge stones. Often they are so delicately balanced, you wonder how some of the stones are still standing!

Stone boxes

Megalithic tombs were built in parts of Scotland, Wales and Ireland, and also in the southwest tip of England, in Cornwall.

A megalithic tomb can be described as a box or chamber made from big stones. Many chambers were made from just three or four huge stones – two or three standing upright with one giant 'capstone' across the top to form the roof.

Once the chamber had been made, it was covered with a mound, or cairn, of smaller stones. There could be thousands of stones in the cairn. The entrance to the chamber was left open, so people could come and go.

Today, most megalithic tombs have lost their covering of cairn stones. Over the years the stones have been taken away to build walls, farm buildings and houses. All that remains are the big stones of the chamber.

Houses of the dead

Archaeologists think megalithic tombs were used in the same way as long barrows, and were shared by groups of people. The tombs were like houses where the dead could carry on living in the prehistoric afterlife.

From time to time, the bones of the dead might have been brought out of the tombs, so they could be amongst living people, before being put back inside.

The Grey Cairns of Camster in Caithness, Scotland, are two of the best preserved Neolithic chambered tombs in Britain.

Four megalithic tombs

Lanyon Quoit, Cornwall, England

This tomb fell down in 1815 and was rebuilt a few years later. Today, the huge capstone, weighing about 12 tonnes, is balanced on top of three upright stones.

Pentre Ifan, Pembrokeshire, Wales

A megalithic tomb with a 16-tonne capstone resting on the tips of three standing stones.

Cairnholy tomb, Kirkudbrightshire, Scotland

If one chamber was not enough, Neolithic people added a second one. They did this at a megalithic tomb at Cairnholy, by building a new chamber in front of the old one. At the same time, they added a semi-circle of tall standing stones at the front, giving the tomb a splendid entrance.

Brownshill dolmen, County Carlow, Ireland

The giant capstone weighs an estimated 100 tonnes and is thought to be the heaviest in Europe.

15

MAES HOWE PASSAGE GRAVE

Some of Britain's best-preserved prehistoric places are on the Orkney Islands, just off the north coast of Scotland. Among them is Maes Howe, a 5,000-year-old tomb and the most intact prehistoric building in the whole of Britain.

Inside Maes Howe. The flat stones were carefully shaped to make the walls smooth.

The name 'Maes Howe' might come from Viking words meaning 'meadow mound'.

Inside the mound

Maes Howe is a passage grave, and it was built to last. From a distance, it looks like a large, round mound completely covered with grass, but inside it is an amazing building made entirely from stone.

The mound is about 7 m high and 35 m across. A long, low passage leads into the centre of the mound – you have to stoop or crawl on your hands and knees to move along it.

The passage leads to a large, square chamber, with three small side chambers leading off from it. Archaeologists think that dead bodies were placed inside the chambers, although they were empty when Maes Howe was first excavated.

The Neolithic builders used large slabs of flat stone to build the tomb. They laid the slabs so that each one jutted out a little from the slab below it. It meant that as the walls of the chamber went up, they gradually sloped in towards the middle. Finally, a single large capstone was placed on top of the walls to make the roof.

On the shortest day

For most of the year the inside of the tomb is in total darkness, but around Midwinter's Day, 21st December, something incredible happens.

At this time of year, as the sun sets, its light shines along the passage and into the chamber: for a few moments, the sun brings light to the chamber's darkness. The tomb builders had carefully lined up the passage and the chamber with the sun.

Archaeologists think Midwinter's Day – the shortest day – was important to prehistoric people. It meant the start of a new year: as the days grew brighter and longer, it must have seemed as if the sun had been born again. Perhaps this is why prehistoric people wanted the sun to shine into Maes Howe, as if new life could be given to those buried inside.

Sunlight shines into Maes Howe around Midwinter.

Viking visitors

In the 800s, Vikings from Norway began to settle on the Orkney Islands. In the 1100s, some of them went inside the abandoned Maes Howe, thinking there was treasure inside (there wasn't)! They scratched their names and messages on the walls. They used short straight lines to make runes, which were the letters of the Viking alphabet. Here's what three of the Viking messages say:

★ 'Haermund Hardaxe carved these runes.'
★ 'Ingigerd is the most beautiful of women.'
★ 'It was long ago that a great treasure was hidden here. Happy is he that might find that great treasure.'

The Vikings also scratched pictures on the walls – there is a dragon, a walrus and a snake coiled up into a knot.

Viking runes scratched inside Maes Howe

BRONZE AGE ROUND BARROWS

Starting about 4,300 years ago, the prehistoric people of Britain started using metal rather than stone. The Bronze Age had begun, and with it came new ideas about tombs, and about how to bury the dead.

Bronze chisel

New tombs for a new age

The tombs of the Bronze Age are very different from the tombs that came before. Rather than building large stone tombs with chambers and passages inside, people started to make smaller ones. They often grouped these tombs together.

Types of Bronze Age round barrow

Archaeologists call Bronze Age tombs 'round barrows'. There are several different types.

Bowl barrow: a simple round mound often surrounded by a ditch.

Bell barrow: like a bowl barrow but with a flat area between the mound and the ditch.

Pond barrow: instead of a mound there's a shallow, round scoop in the ground.

Saucer barrow: a low, flattened mound, like an upturned saucer.

Disc barrow: a small mound surrounded by a ditch and a bank of earth.

Burying the dead

At the start of the Bronze Age, the body of a dead person was usually buried in a crouched position. The legs were bent and the knees were pulled up close to the chin, as if the person was sleeping.

Later, instead of the body being buried, it was burned on a very hot fire. This is called cremation. When the fire went out, the remaining small pieces of burned bone were collected. These pieces were placed inside a container such as a pot or a basket, which was then buried.

A Bronze Age pottery cremation urn. Fragments of burned bone were put inside it, then the urn was buried.

Deepest prehistoric shaft

In 1960, archaeologists excavated a site in Wilsford, Wiltshire, expecting to find a pond barrow. Instead, they found a deep underground shaft. It had been dug by Bronze Age people about 3,400 years ago. The shaft went straight down for 30 m, making it the deepest prehistoric shaft in Britain. At the bottom archaeologists found wooden buckets, rope, pottery and amber beads. Some archaeologists think the shaft was a well, and water was pulled to the surface in buckets. Others say it was a place to throw objects inside, as gifts to the gods.

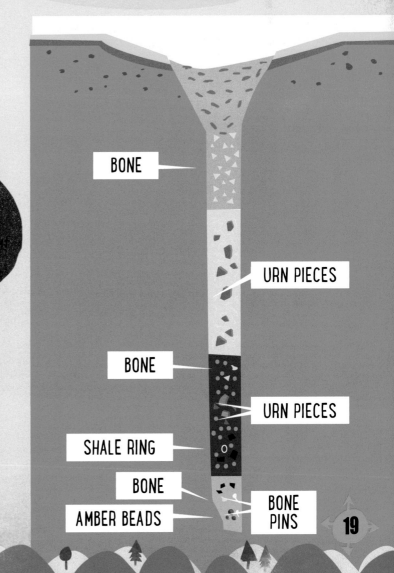

BONE

URN PIECES

BONE

URN PIECES

SHALE RING

BONE

AMBER BEADS

BONE PINS

BUSH BARROW – A CHIEFTAIN'S TOMB?

Near the start of the Bronze Age, an important man was buried inside a round barrow, close to the famous stone circle at Stonehenge. About 4,000 years later, his tomb was opened and fabulous treasure was found. But who was the man?

Barrow grouping

Bronze Age round barrows are found on their own, or in groups. One of the largest barrow groupings in Britain is about one kilometre from Stonehenge. This is the Normanton Down barrow grouping, where about forty round barrows are found close together.

One of the barrows is called 'Bush Barrow', because a clump of trees used to grow on top of it. However, when it was new, the barrow looked like a bright, white mound because it was made from fresh white chalk dug straight from the ground.

Bush Barrow is found in the Normanton Down barrow grouping, near Stonehenge.

Buried treasure

When Bush Barrow was opened in 1808, its secrets were revealed. Inside was the skeleton of a man. He was lying in a crouched position on his left side, and had been buried with precious objects. They included:

★ A gold hook for fastening a belt
★ A large gold breastplate
★ Three bronze daggers
★ A bronze axe
★ A stone macehead

A very important person

The precious objects are a clue that the man was someone special. Because he had been buried with expensive things, archaeologists think he must have been a leader, such as a chieftain or a king.

The man buried inside Bush Barrow had this large gold breastplate sewn to his clothes. It is 18 cm wide.

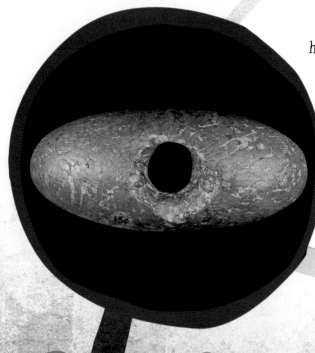

Stone macehead

The stone macehead in the Bush Barrow had been polished to make it smooth, and a hole had been drilled through the middle for a wooden handle. Gold and pieces of bone were attached to the handle. Since so much care had been taken over making it, the macehead might never have been used as a weapon. Instead, it might have been a symbol that declared whoever owned it was a leader.

GIFTS FOR THE AFTERLIFE

Prehistoric people were often buried with objects. Archaeologists call these things 'grave goods'. We can learn a lot from them about the lives of people in the past.

Drawing of a Neolithic pottery bowl

What were grave goods for?

Archaeologists think that prehistoric people believed in an afterlife – a place where their souls carried on living in a new life after death.

To help a person get started in the afterlife, they were buried with lots of everyday items, such as clothes, food, pottery, weapons and jewellery.

A cape made from a thin sheet of gold, found in a Bronze Age grave in Mold, north Wales. It must have belonged to an important person.

What can archaeologists learn from grave goods?

Grave goods can help archaeologists decide if the person was an ordinary person or someone special. For example, someone buried with expensive and rare things was probably an important person, like the man buried inside Bush Barrow.

The materials that grave goods are made from can tell archaeologists if they are dealing with a Stone Age, Bronze Age or Iron Age grave. Pottery is also very useful: prehistoric people made different types of pottery over time, so archaeologists can tell when it was made.

Sometimes archaeologists discover objects that had travelled a long distance before they were buried in the ground, showing that prehistoric people travelled and traded with those who lived far away.

Reconstruction of a Bronze Age man buried with grave goods for the afterlife.

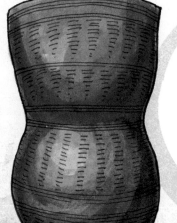

Bronze Age beaker

At the start of the Bronze Age period, people began drinking from pottery beakers. They were highly decorated with patterns. Beakers were often used as grave goods and are found inside Bronze Age round barrows. Archaeologists think they were filled with a drink for the person to enjoy in the afterlife.

THE LAST BARROW BUILDERS

About 2,800 years ago, a new type of metal came into use in Britain. It was iron, a harder and stronger metal than bronze. The Iron Age had begun! The last prehistoric burial mounds were built in the Iron Age — and one of them can be found today in someone's garden.

From Bronze Age to Iron Age

During the Iron Age, the prehistoric people of Britain carried on being farmers, just like their ancestors before them. Farming methods improved, and better varieties of wheat and barley were grown.

However, not everything stayed the same. For example, when Iron Age people died, very few of them were buried in the ground. Something changed between the Bronze Age, when bodies and bones were buried, and the Iron Age, when they weren't.

Where are all the bodies?

There may have been more than one million people living in Iron Age Britain, but archaeologists hardly ever find Iron Age graves. What happened to their bodies after they died?

Human bones are often found at Iron Age sites, in ditches and at the bottom of pits. It makes archaeologists think that dead bodies were left out in the open or placed inside special buildings to rot. Eventually the bones might have been cleared away, which is how they ended up in ditches and pits.

An Iron Age farmer threshing wheat to separate the cereal grains from the ears.

Iron Age barrows in Yorkshire

There's one place in Britain where the bodies of many Iron Age people were buried. It's in the east of Yorkshire, where there are large groups of Iron Age barrows.

When a person died, a pit was dug and the body was placed at the bottom, lying in a crouched position. Weapons, pots, jewellery and food were put around the body. Some people were even buried with chariots.

The pit containing the body and grave goods was filled with soil. Then, a square ditch was dug around the pit. The soil from the ditch was piled up over the pit to make a low mound or barrow, about one metre high.

Iron Age king in Essex

In about 15 BCE, a man was buried beneath a large barrow at Lexden, a district of Colchester, Essex. He must have been important because he was buried with expensive grave goods, including things that had come to Britain from the Romans. Archaeologists wonder if he was the king of a tribe of Iron Age people who lived in this part of Britain. His burial mound was one of the very last made here in prehistoric times. Today the Lexden Barrow, as it's known, is in the back garden of someone's house!

Metal figure of a boar, found inside the Lexden Barrow.

By now, the barrow is just a low mound with trees growing on top of it.

IRON AGE CHARIOT QUEEN

A woman buried 2,300 years ago made news headlines when archaeologists discovered her in 2001. She had been buried beneath a barrow in Yorkshire with a chariot. Was she an Iron Age queen?

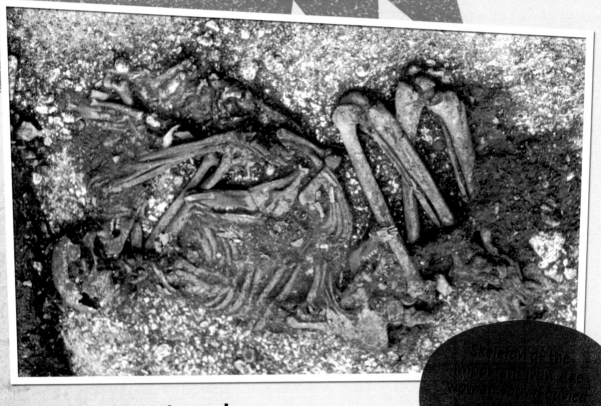

Skeleton of the Iron Age woman found buried at Wetwang.

Buried with a chariot

The barrow was near the village of Wetwang. At the bottom of the burial pit archaeologists uncovered the skeleton of an adult woman.

There were pig bones in her grave from joints of meat. Lying against the woman's ankles was a mirror made from polished bronze. It had a tassel made from hundreds of tiny glass beads.

At her feet were the remains of two large wheels and pieces of horse harness. Around her skeleton were pieces of rusted iron from a large wooden object that had rotted away. From this evidence, archaeologists could see that the woman had been buried with a chariot made from wood and iron.

When bronze is new it's a shiny yellow colour. After it's been buried in the ground for a long time, it turns green.

The iron rims of the chariot wheels were carefully uncovered by archaeologists.

An important woman

She must have been someone important, as ordinary Iron Age women were not buried with chariots and expensive mirrors. Archaeologists have wondered if she was a queen or a princess.

After she died, her body was placed in a deep pit, crouched on her left side. Food for the afterlife and her mirror, which was probably a precious possession, were left with her.

Then, a chariot was taken to pieces and the parts placed around her. The chariot's wooden platform, where the charioteer stood, was placed over her body, and its wheels were at her feet. The chariot might have been to take the woman to the afterlife, and to signal her as a person of importance when she arrived.

The back of an Iron Age mirror

Iron Age mirror

Iron Age mirrors were not like today's glass mirrors. Instead, they were made from a thin piece of bronze which was highly polished so a person's reflection could be seen in it. Some mirrors had intricate patterns on the back. Mirrors were expensive objects, and only the most important people in Iron Age society had them.

THE MYSTERY OF SILBURY HILL

You can't miss the huge mound of Silbury Hill. It was built in the Neolithic period and is the largest prehistoric mound in Europe. It looks as if it should be a burial mound — but is it? Archaeologists are still trying to find out.

From small beginnings

Silbury Hill is in Wiltshire, southwest England. It's close to the West Kennet long barrow and the famous stone circle at Avebury. The cone-shaped mound is 30 m high, and was built in the Neolithic period about 4,400 years ago. At that time it would have stood out as a great white mound because it was built from crushed chalk. Today, it is covered in grass.

Silbury Hill began as a small, low mound of gravel. Then, a great mass of soil and turf was dumped over it, and the mound got bigger. A deep ditch was dug around the mound next, and the soil from the ditch was added to it. As chalk and clay were piled on top, the mound grew and grew. Archaeologists have worked out that it took about 150 years to build Silbury Hill from start to finish.

According to legend, Silbury Hill is where King Sil was buried, dressed in golden armour and seated on a golden horse.

Exploring Silbury Hill

Over the years, many people have dug into Silbury Hill, hoping to find out why it was built. In 1776 miners dug a wide shaft from the top to the bottom. They hoped to find buried treasure, but they came away empty-handed. The shaft was filled in, but not very well.

In 1849, a long tunnel was dug into the side of the hill. Then, in 1968, archaeologists dug a big tunnel to the centre of the mound. It helped them work out when the mound was built, and how, but they still didn't know why.

Saving Silbury Hill

All of these tunnels had damaged Silbury Hill and had made it weak. In 2000, after heavy rain, a deep hole appeared at the top of the hill when the 1776 shaft suddenly opened up. Silbury Hill's stability was in question, so archaeologists quickly explored the hole before filling it.

In 2007, archaeologists decided to check the 1968 tunnel. They found that it too was collapsing. To save Silbury Hill, they filled the tunnel with hundreds of tonnes of chalk, making the mound solid, just as it was when it was built.

Engineers on top of Silbury Hill, exploring the huge hole that had opened up.

The people who built Silbury Hill did it all by hand – it must have been very hard work.

Why was Silbury Hill built?

This is the hardest question to answer. No one has ever found any evidence that it was built as a burial mound. However, as the mound is so big, it may be that archaeologists simply haven't dug in the right place yet. The truth is, no one really knows why Silbury Hill was built. What do you think?

BURIAL PLACES IN NUMBERS

More than **700** Iron Age barrows excavated in East Yorkshire since 1960

300 Neolithic long barrows known to exist

40,000 Bronze Age round barrows scattered all across Britain

30 Viking inscriptions carved inside Maes Howe

15,700 man hours to build the West Kennet long barrow

More than **4,000** Bronze Age round barrows in Wessex (the counties of Wiltshire, Dorset, Hampshire and Berkshire)

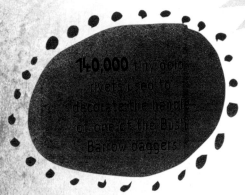

140,000 tiny gold rivets used to decorate the handle of one of the Bush Barrow daggers

379 barrows explored on Salisbury Plain in the early 1800s, including Bush Barrow

500 barrows in one of the Iron Age cemeteries of East Yorkshire

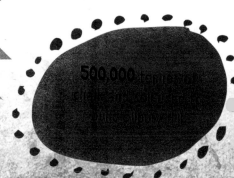

500,000 tonnes

GLOSSARY

afterlife The idea that a person carries on living in a new life after they have died.

archaeologist (say: are-kee-ol-o-jist) A person who finds out about the past, often by digging things up.

barrow A prehistoric burial mound, from an Old English word meaning 'hill'.

beaker A container made from pottery; used to drink from.

bronze A metal made by mixing copper and tin. It's harder than copper, but softer than iron.

burial mound A large heap of soil where the dead were buried.

cairn (say: k-air-n) A mound of stones.

capstone A large, flat stone forming the roof of a burial chamber.

chambered tomb A place with rooms or chambers where the dead were buried in the Neolithic period.

cremation When a dead body is burned on a hot fire until all that is left are small pieces of burned bone.

flint A type of stone that was chipped into shape to make tools such as axes, arrowheads and scrapers.

grave goods Objects left in a grave for a dead person to use in the afterlife.

hunter-gatherer A person who lives by hunting wild animals and gathering wild plants.

macehead The stone or metal top of a mace (a hitting weapon, like a club).

megalithic (say: meg-a-lith-ik) Built from big stones ('mega' means 'big' and 'lithic' means 'stones').

Mesolithic (say: mez-o-lith-ik) The Middle Stone Age period, about 10,000 years ago to 4,000 BCE.

Neolithic (say: nee-o-lith-ik) The New Stone Age period, about 4,000 BCE to 2,300 BCE.

Palaeolithic (say: pal-e-o-lith-ik) The Old Stone Age period, about 800,000 to 10,000 years ago.

prehistory The time in human history before writing began.

roundhouse A circular house made from wattle and daub, wood and thatch.

stone circle A type of monument built in the Neolithic or Bronze Age with standing stones placed in a circle.

thatch A type of roof covering made from straw.

Three Age System A way of dividing prehistory into three parts: Stone Age, Bronze Age and Iron Age.

tumulus (plural: tumuli) A prehistoric burial mound, from a Latin word meaning 'mound' or 'hill'.

wattle and daub Building material made by weaving thin branches (wattles) together and covering them with a thick layer of mud mixed with straw and animal dung (daub).

Understanding dates

• The letters 'BCE' stand for 'Before Common Era'.

• The letters 'CE' stand for 'Common Era'.

• BCE dates are counted backwards from the year 1. CE dates are counted forwards from the year 1. There was no year 0.

• Some dates have a 'c.' in front of them. This stands for 'circa' (say: sur-ka), which means 'about'. These dates are guesses, because no one knows exactly what the real date is.

INDEX

Published in paperback in 2017 by Wayland
Copyright © Hodder and Stoughton, 2017

All rights reserved.

Author: John Malam (johnmalam.co.uk)
Consultant: Mark Bowden, Historic England
Editor: Annabel Stones and Liza Miller

Historic England is a Government service championing England's heritage and giving expert, constructive advice.

ISBN: 9781526303615
10 9 8 7 6 5 4 3 2 1

FSC MIX Paper from responsible sources FSC® C104740
www.fsc.org

Wayland
An imprint of
Hachette Children's Group
Part of Hodder & Stoughton
Carmelite House
50 Victoria Embankment
London EC4Y 0DZ

An Hachette UK Company
www.hachette.co.uk
www.hachettechildrens.co.uk

Printed in China

Cover illustrations © Lee Hodges
images © Crown Copyright Historic Environment Scotland: cover, 16
images © Historic England Publishing: 3l, 3tr, 4r, 6tr, 9t, 10, 11b, 12, 13b, 19t, 20, 22t, 23, 24, 28, 29
images © The Trustees of the British Museum: 3br, 18, 22b, 27b
image © Charles Tait: 17
images © Colchester and ipswich Museums: 25bl, 25br
image © Diego Meozzi: 1
image © Guildhouse, credit Rodney Mackey: 27tl
image © Humber Archaeological Partnership: 25t
image © Kate Dennett: 26, 27tr
illustrations by Kerry Hyndman: 5, 6, 10, 11, 18, 19

Picture credits:
Dreamstime: 8b, 9b, 14;
Old-maps.co.uk: 6tl;
Shutterstock: 4l, 5, 6b, 15;
Wiltshire Museum: 21